MEETING
[GOD]
in
Scripture

Entering the

NEW TESTAMENT

MEETING
[GOD]
in
Scripture

—— *Entering the* ——
NEW TESTAMENT

PARTICIPANT'S
WORKBOOK

UPPER
ROOM BOOKS®
NASHVILLE

MEETING GOD IN SCRIPTURE

Entering the New Testament Participant's Workbook

Copyright © 2008 by Upper Room Books®

All rights reserved.

The Bible book introductions, the entry points, and the article "Reading Scripture Devotionally" originally appeared in *The Spiritual Formation Bible*, New Revised Standard Version, copyright © 1999 by The Zondervan Company. All rights reserved.

The Upper Room® Web site http://www.upperroom.org

UPPER ROOM®, UPPER ROOM BOOKS®, and design logos are trademarks owned by the Upper Room®, a ministry of GBOD®, Nashville, Tennessee. All rights reserved.

Unless otherwise stated, scripture quotations are from the New Revised Standard Version Bible, copyright © 1989 by the Division of Christian Education of the National Council of the Churches of Christ in the U.S.A. Used by permission. All rights reserved.

Cover design: Jade Novak, Anderson Design Group
Cover photos: Shutterstock, iStockPhoto, Photos.com
First printing: 2008

ISBN: 978-0-8358-9967-3

Printed in the United States of America

Contents

Introduction

*W*elcome to *Meeting God in Scripture: Entering the New Testament.* For the next eight weeks, we invite you to explore the New Testament. The Old Testament, commonly called the Hebrew scripture, and the New Testament together comprise the Christian scriptures. You may want to begin your study with *Meeting God in Scripture: Entering the Old Testament* as the New Testament, though valuable in itself, is firmly grounded in the Hebrew scripture. You'll be studying and responding to passages from New Testament scripture in the company of a group of people who, like you, want to learn more about the Bible and the foundational stories of Christian faith.

> **THIS STUDY EMPLOYS A SPIRITUAL FORMATION LENS.**

This is not designed to be a full survey of the New Testament, though you will read passages from most of its books. This study differs both in approach and content. Rather than taking a traditional analytical, outline-and-conquer approach, this study employs a spiritual formation lens. That is, it invites you to "enter into" (respond to) the chosen passages in relation to your life and experiences.

You will read forty passages, one per day for five days during each of the next eight weeks. For every one passage chosen, at least ten others could have had its place. This study omits many wonderful stories and passages; ***its intent is to give you the big picture by offering glimpses of the riches of New Testament scripture***. You will spend three weeks on the synoptic Gospels—Matthew, Mark, and Luke—and the Acts of the Apostles. Readings for weeks four and five come from the Gospel of John and several of the Johannine letters. The next two weeks focus on attributed letters of Paul to young churches in Rome, Corinth, Galatia, Ephesus, Colossae, and Philippi, as well as touching on an epistle to Timothy. The last week's readings come from Hebrews, James, First and Second Peter, and Revelation.

Each reading is accompanied by ***an entry point that focuses on a few verses from the day's passage***. These entry points are simply suggested ways you may enter personally into the Bible's message. The daily readings and entry-point activities will introduce you to the stories and major characters of New Testament scripture. These activities will require no more than ten to fifteen minutes daily. At the end of each week, you will meet with others to reflect on the week's readings and entry points. ***One entry point each week has two stars (**) beside the day.*** Even if you don't have time to do all the readings and responses, try to find time to do this one; it will be used in some way during the weekly meeting. No other preparation for the group meeting is necessary.

This book includes space for your responses to the entry points. Bring it and your Bible with you to the weekly sessions. The leader will tell you about time, place, and format for these meetings.

THE THEME OF THIS STUDY: TRANSFORMED IN CHRIST

The Bible tells the continuing story of God's relationship with humanity and with the people of God. The story begins in the Hebrew scripture with creation and with God's choosing a people, delivering them from slavery, and giving them the law, which defines their relationship with God and with one another. In the New Testament the relationship between God and humanity is focused on the person of Jesus Christ and on the young community of faith in Christ.

In Hebrew scripture, God promises a new world in which all people will live in the presence of God and the sorrows of the present age will be reversed: The lame will walk; the hungry will be fed; the brokenhearted will be comforted (see, for example, Isaiah 61:1-4). God's promised world will be defined by justice, righteousness, mercy, generosity, peace, love. In the New Testament, Jesus comes preaching God's promises, and he makes them happen: He heals the sick, feeds the hungry, raises the dead. He begins to create a community of disciples, who, in their own bumbling ways, try to live the new life God has promised. Jesus Christ embodies the new world. In him, the promises of God are fulfilled.

Living for God's new world, as Jesus did, requires us to change. But none of us is good at being good. Willpower fails us, and faith is seldom strong.

God, in Jesus Christ, assures us that nothing we do can separate us from God's love or keep God's promises from being fulfilled. God accepts our feeble attempts at obedience and brings from them new communities grounded in God's amazing grace.

In relationship with Christ, we are transformed—from corrupt to pure in heart, from false to true, from dead to alive in the love of God.

As you read the New Testament scriptures, encounter the Lord Jesus. Look to him for guidance. Find in him a new way of living. Listen to God's word through scripture, and let it *change you.*

IF YOU WANT TO DO MORE: KEEPING A SPIRITUAL JOURNAL

Keeping a personal journal is a Christian practice that helps seekers attend to God's presence and work in daily life and events. If you have more time to give to this study each day or some days, you may want to write briefly in a journal about your prayers or other responses to the scripture readings. A journal can be a spiral-bound notebook; a file on your computer; or a slightly fancier, bound, blank book that you can find in most bookstores. The journal and what you write in it are private, between you and God. If you keep a journal, bring it with you to group meetings, since you may want to record your responses to some of the group activities. However, *you will never be asked to reveal the contents of your journal to others*; it will remain completely private unless you choose to talk about its contents as part of group discussions.

WHAT GOES IN A JOURNAL?

Anything that you put into your journal is fine. After all, it is yours. You may write a prayer in response to a scripture reading. You may want to draw a picture of some image the reading brings to mind, or you may want to record an idea or insight that you hope to remember. You may write about connections you sense between the Bible's words and your life. If you need help finding something to write about, here are some general questions you can use to journal in response to scripture reading:

- What picture of God do I see in this passage?

- What does this passage tell me about human nature?

- What does this passage reveal about God's ways of dealing with us?

- What connection do I sense between this passage and my life right now?

- What feelings and memories arise as I reflect on this passage?

- What questions does this passage raise for me?

- How does this passage suggest that I might pray?

- What other response does this passage ask of me?

You may copy these questions into the front of your journal. After a while, you will probably find that you don't need the questions because your journal has become like a friend you can talk to easily.

If you're a first-time journaler, ***don't make writing in it a task that has to be done every day***, something to feel guilty about not doing or something that you worry about doing correctly. Even if you write only half a page a week or a month, by the end of the study you will have several pages that you otherwise would not have at all. The value of a spiritual journal is that it helps you pay attention to God. It is not an end in itself.

Reading Scripture Devotionally

The moment we open a book, a powerful set of habitual practices begins to work. Our culture teaches us learning methods that establish the reader as the controlling power who seeks to master the text in order to use it for his or her own purposes. The cognitive, analytical aspects of our beings are hyperdeveloped in our culture; we tend to think that the sharper we are intellectually, the smarter we are, the more quickly we grasp concepts and synthesize them, the more balanced we are.

Responding to God with our whole being entails loving God with all of our mind and using our cognitive abilities. We cannot shirk this aspect. Jesus, however, puts loving God with the heart and soul higher on his list: "'Love the Lord your God with all your heart and with all your soul and with all your mind'" (Matt. 22:37). Loving God with heart and soul precedes loving God with mind. Listing

> LOVING GOD
> WITH HEART AND SOUL
> PRECEDES LOVING
> GOD WITH MIND.

"mind" last doesn't make it less important but implies that it is not the only way to respond to God—or even the dominant way to respond as our culture asserts. (All three synoptic Gospels [see Mark 12:30; Luke 10:27] employ the same order.)

CHARACTERISTICS OF FORMATIONAL SCRIPTURE READING

Our culture's predominant mode of response, however, is often the rational, cognitive, and intellectual. *When this mind-set becomes our only mode of reading scripture, we may find it difficult to have "ears to hear"* (Mark 4:9, 23; Luke 8:8; 14:35). When the mind is our primary filter for scripture, our approach can create an imbalance. We can easily read scripture in a purely cognitive way and decide that this passage doesn't apply to us. (We frequently even pick out some other troublesome person who should obviously heed this text instead of ourselves!) This purely cognitive way of reading insulates the "door" of our being against God's "knocking." Why? We are not really opening our being at deeper levels to the possibility of meeting God in that passage.

What if God wishes to meet us in the passage in an intimate way, according to God's wisdom, communicating what we need to hear but wish to avoid? Allowing God's word to speak transformationally to the deepest levels of our being invites us to develop another way of reading.

FORMATIONAL SCRIPTURE READING

Formational scripture reading differs from our usual approach. Formational scripture reading invites us to open ourselves, allowing God to set the agenda for our lives through the text. It facilitates genuine spiritual formation—the process of being conformed to the image of Jesus Christ. ***Reading formationally helps us open our "rational filter," which can sift out so much of God's voice.*** We begin to hear at the heart-and-soul level. Jesus frequently reminded people of the importance of having "ears to hear" (Mark 4:9, 23; Luke 8:8; 14:35).

Formational reading can help us develop those ears to hear. Let me share a personal experience of formational reading. I was following a prescribed plan for Bible reading and had come to the Exodus event. I'd read about the struggle between God and Pharaoh many times but only informationally. As I read the daily assigned portion, I sat before it and said, ***"Lord, what are you seeking to say to me through this?"*** All sorts of thoughts went through my mind—who said what, Pharaoh's resistance, God's hardening Pharaoh's heart. I got nothing from the text after wrestling with it for a week or more. Finally, each day's portion moved one by one through the ten plagues. I was met each time with silence—or my own noisy understanding of the passage. As I moved toward the end of the passage about the plagues and asked that same question, an answer came: "You are Pharaoh!" "What?" I replied. "Me, Pharaoh? Moses, perhaps, even one of the Hebrews, but Pharaoh? Perhaps a servant or slave, but Pharaoh?" Possibilities began to open up in the text and inside me. I realized that God had given me certain gifts, abilities, and personality traits. All these were God's "children," but I had enslaved them to my own purposes, desires, intentions, and plans. Truly I was the Pharaoh of my life! I came to the last plague—the death of the firstborn. I saw that for me to cease to be Pharaoh in my life, there had to be a death of my "firstborn" desires to use God's gifts for my own purposes. To liberate those gifts for God's use in my life, I would have to cease to be Pharaoh.

Depth. Informational reading seeks to cover as much material as possible as quickly as possible, while formational reading involves smaller portions of scripture. The point is not just to get through the text but to become personally involved in it. Formational reading is concerned with depth, so we may find ourselves "holding on" to just one sentence or paragraph or page for quite a while. We allow the passage to open out to us its deeper dynamics and multiple layers of meaning. **We let the text intrude into our life and address us.**

Openness. In formational reading, **we let the text master us.** We come to the text with an openness to hear, to receive, and to respond. This may feel risky because it lays us open to unforeseen conclusions.

Humility. Formational reading requires a humble approach, a new inner posture in which we willingly relinquish our insights and purposes. We stand before scripture and await its address.

Mystery. Informational reading can be characterized by a problem-solving mentality. When we do respond, we often read our needs and desires into the scripture, asking, **Does this passage solve my problems, answer my questions, meet my needs?** Formational reading invites us to become open to the whole mystery of God. We allow God to address us however God wishes. Eventually, we may discover that problem-solving dynamics emerge from the encounter, but we relinquish the right to solve our problems with scripture.

SUGGESTIONS FOR FORMATIONAL SCRIPTURE READING

Make listening for God's voice a top priority. Focus your attention on what God is saying to you as you read. Listen for God to speak to you in and through, around and within, over and behind the words. Keep asking yourself, "What is God seeking to say to me in all of this?" Allow the text to become an instrument of God's voice in your life. Respond to what you read with your heart and spirit.

Let your response take place down in the deeper levels of your being. Ask yourself questions such as: How do I feel about what is being said? How am I reacting? How am I responding down deep within myself? What is going on inside of me? Then begin to ask yourself "why" questions: *Why* do I feel this way? *Why* am I responding in this manner? *Why* do I have these feelings within?

Let this exercise be *an opportunity to get in touch with the deeper layers of your being*. What do your reactions tell you about your habits, your attitudes, your perspectives, your responses, and your reactions to life? Are you beginning to see something about yourself? Thomas à Kempis said, *"A humble knowledge of ourselves is a surer way to God than is the search for depth of learning."* That humble knowledge of yourself can come when you read scripture if you balance your cognitive response pattern with this affective response from deep within your being.

Prepare to read by quieting yourself. You can't run in, sit down, pick up the text, and read scripture formationally. You have to "center down," to use the old Quaker phrase—*become still, relinquish your agenda, and acknowledge the presence of God*. You may have to relax first in order to do this. When you center yourself in this way, you may find that no word addresses you out of that text on that day, but the constant discipline of preparing yourself and entering into formational reading will itself be spiritually forming to your soul.

Allow the two kinds of reading—informational and formational—to work together. You may begin reading a scripture passage with informational dynamics, but then you must be sensitive to the need to move to the formational dynamics of reading. Allow yourself to become open and receptive to the intrusion of the living Word of God into your garbled, distorted self. You may get tripped up on an informational point and need to move back to an informational mode. There is a necessary interplay between these two approaches, but *you'll ultimately need to arrive at a disciplined development of the formational mode of approaching the text.* As we become skilled at shifting to that inner posture of becoming listeners, we develop "ears to hear." We become receptive and accessible to being addressed by the living Word of God.

—M. Robert Mulholland Jr.

Shaped by God

Read Genesis 1:1-31 and 2:1-8. Read again Genesis 2:7.

These passages offer us a wonderful image of the way God forms us both physically and spiritually. As you held the clay, feeling the weight and temperature, noticing its pliability, working with it, how did you make it

ENTRY POINT:

"God Forms Us"

into a particular form? Based on this exercise, what do you think spiritual formation means? How is God molding or forming you continually, even today? How do you resist or receive God's attention? Note your thoughts on this page.

Genesis 2:7

Then the Lord God formed man from the dust of the ground, and breathed into his nostrils the breath of life; and the man became a living being.

Blessed in the

Promises of God

Day 1

Read the introduction to the book of Matthew on page 67.

Read Matthew 2:1-12. Read again Matthew 2:2.

The wise men come to worship Jesus.

Later others come to him for healing and forgiveness, to learn from him, or in hopes of gaining material blessings or power. Imagine you are a contemporary of Jesus and you have just heard about him. Who told you about Jesus? What did that person say about Jesus? What was the first thing you said? What did you think about just before falling asleep that night? What do you seek now? Ask God to help you find it. Or ask God to teach you, as you read this Gospel, what you should be seeking.

[
ENTRY POINT:
Reasons of the Heart
]

Matthew 2:2

"Where is the child who has been born king of the Jews? For we observed his star at its rising, and have come to pay him homage."

Day 2

Read Matthew 4:1-4. Read again Matthew 4:1-4.

After forty days of fasting, Jesus' need for food was understandably acute. Satan uses this legitimate need to tempt Jesus to "prove" his significance and power. Temptation often results from such legitimate needs.

[ENTRY POINT:

The Temptation of Legitimate Needs]

What needs do you have in your life that aren't being met? Are you tempted to meet those needs in illegitimate ways? Put yourself in Jesus' sandals; imagine his hunger after a forty-day fast. Consider fasting for a day to experience more fully the kinds of sensations Jesus did. How can the strength Jesus exhibits and words he speaks encourage you?

Matthew 4:1-4

Then Jesus was led up by the Spirit into the wilderness to be tempted by the devil. He fasted forty days and forty nights, and afterwards he was famished. The tempter came and said to him, "If you are the Son of God, command these stones to become loaves of bread."

But he answered, "It is written, 'One does not live by bread alone, but by every word that comes from the mouth of God.'"

Day 3**

Read Matthew 5:1-12. Read again Matthew 5:3-10.

If every member of your community made a concerted effort to become poor in spirit, meek, merciful, pure in heart, and prone to promoting peace, how would your community be transformed? How do these

[
ENTRY POINT:

Life with Others
]

beatitudes bring people together? Reflect on this passage by looking at the harm done by the opposite attitudes. What usually follows in the wake of a haughty spirit? What happens when people become demanding? divisive? critical? How can God use you in your church, circle of friends, or neighborhood to reflect the character of the spirit of Jesus?

Matthew 5:3-10

"Blessed are the poor in spirit, for theirs is the kingdom of heaven.

"Blessed are those who mourn, for they will be comforted.

"Blessed are the meek, for they will inherit the earth.

"Blessed are those who hunger and thirst for righteousness, for they will be filled.

"Blessed are the merciful, for they will receive mercy.

"Blessed are the pure in heart, for they will see God.

"Blessed are the peacemakers, for they will be called children of God.

"Blessed are those who are persecuted for righteousness; sake, for theirs is the kingdom of heaven."

Day 4

Read Matthew 5:43-48. Read again Matthew 5:44.

One thing that set Jesus' teaching so radically apart from that of religious leaders is that the religious leaders emphasized what people shouldn't do while Jesus stressed the positive nature of our calling—what we

ENTRY POINT:

A Positive Ethic

should do. It's not enough to refrain from killing our enemies; we are called to love them and pray for them. Think about your own shortcomings and how you might counteract each one with a positive virtue. For example, instead of being critical, learn to encourage; instead of hoarding wealth, learn to be generous, and so on. Ask God to help you go beyond merely desiring change to being transformed into his likeness.

Matthew 5:44

"But I say to you, Love your enemies and pray for those who persecute you."

Day 5

Read Matthew 9:35-38. Read again Matthew 9:35.

As Jesus walks through Judea, he brings people back from the dead, heals others of long-standing diseases, frees some from demons, and freely offers the wonderful news that God is at work in the world. He

[
ENTRY POINT:

Pouring Light into Darkness
]

dismantles hell every step of the way, destroying it with the word and works of God.

Your daily passage through the streets to your office and your home may not be quite so dramatic; but how, realistically, can you help to bring God's kingdom? Start by taking notice of the people around you. Become aware of their needs for compassion and for God's love and truth. How can you bring God's light into dark situations as the Holy Spirit works through you?

Matthew 9:35

Then Jesus went about all the cities and villages, teaching in their synagogues, and proclaiming the good news of the kingdom, and curing every disease and every sickness.

Coming before Christ

As Is

Day 1

Read the introduction to the book of Mark on page 68.

Read Mark 4:35-41. Read again Mark 4:38-39.

Whether it's a family estrangement, a church dispute, or a national disaster, we sometimes

find ourselves asking, "God, don't you care . . . ?" Imagine

[
ENTRY POINT:

**To Trust
or Not to
Trust**
]

yourself on this life-threatening voyage. You've bailed water for hours. Your legs are bruised from being banged about the boat by the heaving waves. You are cold, wet, and bone-weary. With a hoarse voice you ask, "Teacher, do you not care . . . ?"

What about this passage touches you the most? That Jesus could control an uncontrollable force? That Jesus was surprised by their fear? That the disciples expected Jesus to intervene, but then, when he did, were astounded that he could help? What does this passage say to you about the mystery of God's presence in seemingly uncontrollable circumstances?

Mark 4:38-39

But [Jesus] was in the stern, asleep on the cushion; and they woke him up and said to him, "Teacher, do you not care that we are perishing?" He woke up and rebuked the wind, and said to the sea, "Peace! Be still!" Then the wind ceased, and there was a dead calm.

*Day 2***

Read Mark 10:17-31. Read again Mark 10:21-27.

The dashing young star of this passage is

also a meticulously religious person. Jesus pierces his heart, however, by demanding that he surrender the wealth and position that he values more than God.

ENTRY POINT:

All Things Are Possible

Imagine yourself face-to-face with Jesus. You are self-possessed, well-mannered, surrounded by your accomplishments. Your motives are honorable. Imagine Jesus looking into your eyes so that you know the depth of his love for you. Now imagine him asking you to give up something that is very precious to you. You cringe. "O Lord, not that!" Now Jesus is telling you that all things are possible with God. What do you need to say to God in response?

Mark 10:21-27

Jesus, looking at him, loved him and said, "You lack one thing; go, sell what you own, and give the money to the poor, and you will have treasure in heaven; then come, follow me." When he heard this, he was shocked and went away grieving, for he had many possessions.

Then Jesus looked around and said to his disciples, "How hard it will be for those who have wealth to enter the kingdom of God!" And the disciples were perplexed at these words. But Jesus said to them again, "Children, how hard it is to enter the kingdom of God! It is easier for a camel to go through the eye of a needle than for someone who is rich to enter the kingdom of God." They were greatly astounded and said to one another, "Then who can be saved?" Jesus looked at them and said, "For mortals it is impossible, but not for God; for God all things are possible."

Day 3

Read the introduction to the book of Luke on page 69.

Read Luke 8:11-15. Read again Luke 8:15.

Attending to God's voice requires effort.
We're so unaccustomed to listening that we often let God's messages go unnoticed. Or we hear God speaking to us,

[
ENTRY POINT:

Letting the Word Grow
]

but we don't let the words take root in our inner being. Pleasures and problems quickly overshadow them. What does it say about God's nature that God continues to plant seeds even though people don't nurture them? What does it say about our human nature that we're so easily distracted? What do you want to say to God or ask God about these issues? What does this passage tell you that you need to do in order to hear God better?

Luke 8:15

"But as for that in the good soil, these are the ones who, when they hear the word, hold it fast in an honest and good heart, and bear fruit with patient endurance."

Day 4

Read Luke 10:38-42. Read again Luke 10:41-42.

Put yourself in Martha's place. You have worked hard to offer the Lord hospitality, using all the skills you have and providing the sumptuous feast that is fitting for your honored guest. Hot and tired, your face

ENTRY POINT:

"Lord, Don't You Care?"

contorts with annoyance when you see Mary just sitting at Jesus' feet. You ask, "Lord, do you not care that my sister has left me to do all the work by myself?"

Let Jesus address you lovingly, personally: "_____, you are worried and distracted by many things." Tell Jesus "the many things" bothering you. Hear Jesus say to you: "_____, there is need of only one thing." What is the one thing that's needed now in life? Allow a word or phrase to rise within you. Repeat it slowly, letting that word or phrase carry your concerns, one by one, into the heart of God.

Luke 10:41-42

But the Lord answered her, "Martha, Martha, you are worried and distracted by many things; there is need of only one thing. Mary has chosen the better part, which will not be taken away from her."

Read Luke 15:11-32. Read again Luke 15:31-32.

Read this passage silently and create an "inner video" of it.

Converse with each character: the younger prodigal son; the angry, perfectionist older son; the heartbroken father; and the unseen mother. With whom do you identify most? Why? Return to the older sibling, identifying your own dutiful, resentful feelings. Hear God's reassuring words: "You are always with me." God invites you to claim your inheritance: "All that is mine is yours." Repeat these empowering words. Let them become your prayer of thanksgiving as you offer yourself to God: "You are always with me, and all that is mine is yours."

[
ENTRY POINT:

Reassuring Words, Empowering Words
]

Luke 15:31-32

Then the father said to him, "Son, you are always with me, and all that is mine is yours. But we had to celebrate and rejoice, because this brother of yours was dead and has come to life; he was lost and has been found."

Encountering Christ in His Death and

Resurrection

Day 1

Read Matthew 27:32-56. Read again Matthew 27:33, 45-50.

Imagine that you are standing on Golgotha while Jesus is being crucified. Look around you. Listen to the sound of the hammer pounding nails into soft flesh, the thud of the cross as it is lifted into position. Look at

[
ENTRY POINT:

At the Cross
]

the people there with you. Some are mocking, some weeping. What are you doing? Do you talk to others or keep to yourself? What are your thoughts and feelings as the sky grows dark and as Jesus cries out?

Sing a hymn such as "Go to Dark Gethsemane," "When I Survey the Wondrous Cross," or "Were You There." What emotions do you experience as you sing? How have you encountered the reality of Jesus' death through these hymns?

Matthew 27:33, 45-50

They came to a place called Golgotha (which means Place of a Skull). . . .

From noon on, darkness came over the whole land until three in the afternoon. And about three o'clock Jesus cried with a loud voice, "Eli, Eli, lema sabachthani?" that is, "My God, my God, why have you forsaken me?" When some of the bystanders heard it, they said, "This man is calling for Elijah." At once one of them ran and got a sponge, filled it with sour wine, put it on a stick, and gave it to him to drink. But the others said, "Wait, let us see whether Elijah will come to save him." Then Jesus cried again with a loud voice and breathed his last.

Day 2**

Read Mark 16:1-8. Read again Mark 16:4-8.

Meeting an angel is so shocking to this group of women that they leave the garden trembling and bewildered. Even though Jesus had told them to expect his resurrection, they are still astounded at what the angel has told them.

ENTRY POINT:

Encountering the Unexpected

Read the passage slowly and sit quietly. Wait in silence, being content to enjoy God's Word. What word, phrase, or image impresses you and stays with you? Reflect on this word or phrase. Why do you think it is important? What is God's message to you? How will you respond when you meet him unexpectedly? Ask God what you need to learn from this passage.

Mark 16:4-8

When [the women] looked up, they saw that the stone, which was very large, had already been rolled back. As they entered the tomb, they saw a young man, dressed in a white robe, sitting on the right side; and they were alarmed. But he said to them, "Do not be alarmed; you are looking for Jesus of Nazareth, who was crucified. He has been raised; he is not here. Look, there is the place they laid him. But go, tell his disciples and Peter that he is going ahead of you to Galilee; there you will see him, just as he told you." So they went out and fled from the tomb, for terror and amazement had seized them; and they said nothing to anyone, for they were afraid.

Read the introduction to the book of Acts on page 71.

Read Acts 2:1-12. Read again Acts 2:1-4.

How do you picture the Holy Spirit? Here the Spirit is likened to a violent wind and tongues of fire.

[
ENTRY POINT:

Your Picture of the Spirit
]

In Matthew 3:16 the Spirit is compared to a descending dove. Elsewhere the Spirit is experienced through various gifts (see 1 Corinthians 12:4-11) and fruit (see Galatians 5:22-23). Try praising God with your hands as you draw or paint your own image or images of the Spirit.

Acts 2:1-4

When the day of Pentecost had come, they were all together in one place. And suddenly from heaven there came a sound like the rush of a violent wind, and it filled the entire house where they were sitting. Divided tongues, as of fire, appeared among them, and a tongue rested on each of them. All of them were filled with the Holy Spirit and began to speak in other languages, as the Spirit gave them ability.

Read Acts 9:1-19. Read again Acts 9:13-16.

Ananias is afraid to go to Saul (Paul)

because he knows only who Saul has been, not who he is becoming since his encounter with Jesus Christ. You might try drawing simple cartoons to illustrate the "before" and "after"

ENTRY POINT:

Before and After

versions of Paul. What are the outward changes? How might you illustrate the inward ones? What if you were to try the same exercise with yourself? What changes has Jesus made in your life? What is still

"in process"? You might go even further and illustrate the "ideal you" that you are becoming in Jesus.

Acts 9:13-16

But Ananias answered, "Lord, I have heard from many about this man, how much evil he has done to your saints in Jerusalem; and here he has authority from the chief priests to bind all who invoke your name." But the Lord said to him, "Go, for he is an instrument whom I have chosen to bring my name before Gentiles and kings and before the people of Israel; I myself will show him how much he must suffer for the sake of my name."

Read Acts 10:1-35. Read again Acts 10:34-35.

"I truly understand that God shows no partiality, but in every nation anyone who fears him and does what is right is acceptable to him." What an amazing statement! Turn this sentence over and over in your mind.

ENTRY POINT:

Who Is Acceptable?

Mull it over until you have extracted all its truth. Take it in little bites: no partiality . . . every nation . . . is acceptable. What do you learn about God's love? What call do you hear to change your attitude toward others? What good news do you hear for yourself?

Acts 10:34-35

Then Peter began to speak to them: "I truly understand that God shows no partiality, but in every nation anyone who fears him and does what is right is acceptable to him."

A New Creation in *Christ*

Day 1 * *

Read the introduction to the book of John on page 70.

Read John 1:1-18. Read again John 1:1-5.

John's rich, resonating words sound out like a majestic overture. Imagine trumpets and drums as the great themes of this Gospel are declared: "In the

[
ENTRY POINT:

A Light Shines
]

beginning was the Word"; "in him was life"; "the light shines"; "darkness did not overcome it." As you walk around the room, read this passage again aloud, as loudly as the text suggests to you. As you read, listen for a word or phrase that catches your attention. Repeat it and let it expand within your spirit. Sense its power. Give it the center stage of your consciousness and let it speak. When you are ready, let this experience serve as the foundation for a prayer of reflection.

John 1:1-5

In the beginning was the Word, and the Word was with God, and the Word was God. He was in the beginning with God. All things came into being through him, and without him not one thing came into being. What has come into being in him was life, and the life was the light of all people. The light shines in the darkness, and the darkness did not overcome it.

 *Day 2*

Read John 2:1-11. Read again John 2:6-10.

Sometimes the things God asks us to do just don't seem to make sense! Jesus says, "Fill the jars with water." But why fill up the jars with water when it is wine that has run out? Even though it seems to make no

ENTRY POINT:

Doing What Jesus Says

sense, the servants do as they are told. The water becomes premium wine. The hosts experience honor rather than shame.

You may ask, "What am I running out of? What shortages are my family, my faith community, or my neighborhood likely to encounter?" Tell Jesus about them. What does Jesus ask you to do in response? What act of obedience does Jesus ask of you so that the situation might be transformed? What do you envision Jesus doing as you cooperate with him?

John 2:6-10

Now standing there were six stone water—jars for the Jewish rites of purification, each holding twenty or thirty gallons. Jesus said to them, "Fill the jars with water." And they filled them up to the brim. He said to them, "Now draw some out, and take it to the chief steward." So they took it. When the steward tasted the water that had become wine, and did not know where it came from (though the servants who had drawn the water knew), the steward called the bridegroom and said to him, "Everyone serves the good wine first, and then the inferior wine after the guests have become drunk. But you have kept the good wine until now."

Day 3

Read John 3:1-9. Read again John 3:1-3.

Nicodemus admires Jesus and has many questions to ask, but he has much to lose—security, position, and power—if he is public about his admiration, so he seeks Jesus under the cover of darkness. Yet Jesus asks the

[
ENTRY POINT:

You
Choose
]

Pharisee to do something much more profound and much more difficult than putting his lifestyle in jeopardy—he asks him to be "born from above."

Ask the Spirit to bless your imagination and your senses as you take your place in the story as Nicodemus. What is happening? What do you see? What do you hear—around you and from Jesus? Smell the evening air. Feel the breeze. Ask Jesus to speak to you about your fears and questions. Ask what being "born from above" could mean for you right now. Let Jesus enlighten your lack of understanding, your stubborn resistance, or your glad acceptance. Carry the experience in your heart during the coming week.

John 3:1-3

Now there was a Pharisee named Nicodemus, a leader of the Jews. He came to Jesus by night and said to him, "Rabbi, we know that you are a teacher who has come from God; for no one can do these signs that you do apart from the presence of God." Jesus answered him, "Very truly, I tell you, no one can see the kingdom of God without being born from above."

Read John 4:7-15. Read again John 4:13-15.

Walk around the room as you read verses 13 through 15 aloud three times. Put the Bible down, and walk around the room again, reciting the text three more times. Now, seated comfortably, with this text and a glass of

ENTRY POINT:
Living Water

water in front of you, name your thirsts. Pray the same request that the Samaritan woman made of Jesus: "Sir, give me this water." Drink the water as you receive Jesus' gift, a spring of water that gushes up to eternal life. Rest in God's presence. As you go out into the world, let the water of eternal life flow through your heart and out to others through your words and actions.

John 4:13-15

Jesus said to her, "Everyone who drinks of this water will be thirsty again, but those who drink of the water that I will give them will never be thirsty. The water that I will give will become in them a spring of water gushing up to eternal life." The woman said to him, "Sir, give me this water, so that I may never be thirsty or have to keep coming here to draw water."

Day 5

Read John 10:7-18. Read again John 10:11-15.

Jesus is the good shepherd. The shepherd cares for you.

He knows your name. He will protect you and guard you from those who want to destroy you. And he knows the path that lies ahead of you.

[ENTRY POINT:

The Good Shepherd]

What is ahead of you right now? With crayon or paint, draw or paint a picture of it. Are you walking into green pastures or dark valleys? Draw Jesus in your picture. Think about the implications of Jesus' presence. Envisioning Jesus ahead of you as you walk, pray about what is happening to you.

John 10:11-15

"I am the good shepherd. The good shepherd lays down his life for the sheep. The hired hand, who is not the shepherd and does not own the sheep, sees the wolf coming and leaves the sheep and runs away—and the wolf snatches them and scatters them. The hired hand runs away because a hired hand does not care for the sheep. I am the good shepherd. I know my own and my own know me, just as the Father knows me and I know the Father. And I lay down my life for the sheep."

New Life in

Christ

Day 1

Read John 11:17-27. Read again John 11:21-26.

Jesus is "the resurrection and the life." Is your perception of the future determined by the certainty of your death or by your faith in Jesus? Is your life determined by the ability to make life "happen" or by the

[
ENTRY POINT:

Resurrection and Life
]

power of Jesus' presence within you to give you life? Find a quiet place and a quiet moment. Quiet your body and slowly breathe the life of Jesus' presence in. Hold your breath and let your mind and heart say, "Jesus, my life!" Slowly breathe "death" out. Hold your breath and let your mind and heart say, "Jesus, my resurrection!" Repeat these phrases a few times. Let Jesus speak to you of resurrection and life.

John 11:21-26

Martha said to Jesus, "Lord, if you had been here, my brother would not have died. But even now I know that God will give you whatever you ask of him." Jesus said to her, "Your brother will rise again." Martha said to him, "I know that he will rise again in the resurrection on the last day." Jesus said to her, "I am the resurrection and the life. Those who believe in me, even though they die, will live, and everyone who lives and believes in me will never die. Do you believe this?"

Read John 14:1-7. Read again John 14:1.

"'Do not let your hearts be troubled.'" Jesus is saying we can trust him.

He is telling us to "believe" in God—not a generic "god" but "the Father" to whom he leads us. We make a choice to trust him and the

[
ENTRY POINT:
Troubles and Trust
]

Father to bear our troubles for us.

So what is troubling you? Feel the intensity of that problem. Listen to its demands. Face its immensity and offer it in complete abandonment to God. Pray, "Lord, I choose you." Take the prayer with you and repeat it many times. Let God shoulder your trouble. Jesus is promising that you will not be orphaned and left to face your troubles alone.

John 14:1

"Do not let your hearts be troubled. Believe in God, believe also in me."

Read John 15:1-11. Read again John 15:5.

Draw a vine. Watch each branch grow
under your pencil. Note that no branch is more
important than another. Each branch is dependent on the
main stem. Let your vine do what vines are supposed to do,

ENTRY POINT:

Bearing Fruit

and draw some fruit growing from
the branch that passes on all the
necessary nutrients from the vine.
Grounded in the self-giving love of
Jesus, the true vine, talk with other
people in your faith community
about an action you can take together that will show love as
visibly as fruit.

John 15:5

"I am the vine, you are the branches. Those who
abide in me and I in them bear much fruit,
because apart from me you can do nothing."

Day 4**

Read the introduction to the book of First John on page 89.

Read 1 John 3:16-18. Read again 1 John 3:16-18.

Many people think they know something when in reality they only know *about* it. They are limited by secondhand knowledge—a poor substitute for the real thing!

[
ENTRY POINT:

Love in Action
]

We know the love of Jesus Christ because he laid down his life for us. And John reminds us that the best way to experience that love is to express it. How might you demonstrate that love to God? How might you demonstrate love to those who are closest to you; to your friends or associates at work, school, church; to those who are in need or maybe even to a person you don't particularly like? Create a symbol or reminder to encourage you to make love visible to others. Carry it with you, or place it on your mirror or in another prominent spot.

1 John 3:16-18

We know love by this, that he laid down his life for us—and we ought to lay down our lives for one another. How does God's love abide in anyone who has the world's goods and sees a brother or sister in need and yet refuses help?

Little children, let us love, not in word or speech, but in truth and action.

Read the introduction to the book of Third John on page 91.

Read 3 John 2-4. Read again 3 John 2.

Our society is health conscious, a phenomenon

that is clearly confirmed by the number of health publications, vitamins and supplements, kinds of exercise equipment, and assorted experimental healing techniques that are available on the market. And modern medicine is finally discovering the reality that scripture has consistently communicated: the

> ENTRY POINT:
>
> # The Source of True Health

connection between the health of our spirit and the health of our bodies. We rarely hear, however, that one of the basic principles of a healthful life is truth!

When our lives are characterized by honesty and integrity, we reduce the need to conceal or deceive. Our level of peace goes up, and our stress level goes down. Jesus was telling the gospel truth when he reminded us that the truth sets us free (see John 8:32). Where do you most need this freedom in your life? How are you being challenged to walk in greater truth? Spend some moments quietly seeking and listening to God's Spirit. If possible, share your insights with a trusted friend who can pray with you and encourage you to walk in the truth.

3 John 2

Beloved, I pray that all may go well with you and that you may be in good health, just as it is well with your soul.

Amazing

Grace

Day 1

Read the introduction to the book of Romans on page 72.

Read Romans 5:6-8. Read again Romans 5:8.

Our consumer-driven culture tempts us to speak glibly about sacrifice and self-denial: "I'd give my right arm for tickets to that game." "That ice cream is to die for." Do we take in the amazing reality of such wondrous love—that Jesus not only offered to die for us, but he actually did? If we fully absorbed this truth, would we not walk day by day in awe?

[
ENTRY POINT:

The Gift of Life
]

Repeat verse 8 slowly, personalizing it: "While I was still a sinner, Christ died for me." Can you understand why? Would you die for someone else? Would you willingly take the punishment someone else deserved? What kind of connection would you have to have with someone to put yourself in that person's place? Write a letter to the One who died for you, expressing what you think and feel about his wondrous sacrifice for you.

Romans 5:8

God proves his love for us in that while we still
were sinners Christ died for us.

Read Romans 7:15, 21-25; 8:1-2. Read again Romans 7:15; 8:1-2

Paul was no stranger to the struggle

against the sinful nature. He knew what it was like to want to do one thing and yet do another. On a daily basis we fall short of being who God wants us to be and of doing what God wants us to do.

[
ENTRY POINT:

The Reality of Struggle
]

In what area of your life have you experienced continual struggle, perhaps for years? Tell God about your struggles. End your prayer by reading Romans 8:1-2 as God's promise to you. Ask God's Spirit to live in you, and find some object to carry with you as a reminder of the Spirit within you—a cross, a small rock, a written verse from scripture. Keep this symbol where you can touch it when you need to remember that you live by grace.

Romans 7:15; 8:1-2

I do not understand my own actions. For I do not do what I want, but I do the very thing I hate. . . . There is therefore now no condemnation for those who are in Christ Jesus. For the law of the Spirit of life in Christ Jesus has set you free from the law of sin and of death.

Day 3

Read Romans 8:35-39. Read again Romans 8:38-39.

"Can a woman forget her nursing child, or show no compassion for the child of her womb? Even these may forget, yet I will not forget you. See, I have inscribed you on the palms of my hands" (Isa. 49:15-16).

[
ENTRY POINT:
Utterly
Inseparable
]

Find an old tree whose roots are deeply entwined with the earth and with other roots, or find moss that has grown on a tree trunk. Or at the beach find a shell that has attached itself to a rock. Look for other examples of such deep inseparability. As you hold or look at these objects, speak the words of this passage, using them as a description for the One who holds you close.

Romans 8:38-39

For I am convinced that neither death, nor life, nor angels, nor rulers, nor things present, nor things to come, nor powers, nor height, nor depth, nor anything else in all creation, will be able to separate us from the love of God in Christ Jesus our Lord.

Day 4

Read the introduction to the book of First Corinthians on page 73.

Read 1 Corinthians 12:4-26. Read again 1 Corinthians 12:4-6, 13, 26

Paul proposes that unity in diversity is central to life in the Christian community.

He sees in the community different gifts but the same Spirit; different

[
ENTRY POINT:

Unity in Diversity
]

services and deeds but the same God working through them; an array of people called to be baptized—Jews and Greeks, slaves and free—who are part of the same body. How might the words of this passage

influence the way you relate to people in the church? the way in which you pray? To bring the message of Paul closer to home, name someone you know who is suffering. Think of another person who has recently been honored or acknowledged in some way. Think of someone who exhibits each of the spiritual gifts listed in verses 8 through 10.

1 Corinthians 12:4-6, 13, 26

Now there are varieties of gifts, but the same Spirit; and there are varieties of services, but the same Lord; and there are varieties of activities, but it is the same God who activates all of them in everyone. . . . For in the one Spirit we were all baptized into one body—Jews or Greeks, slaves or free—and we were all made to drink of one Spirit. . . . If one member suffers, all suffer together with it; if one member is honored, all rejoice together with it.

Day 5

Read the introduction to the book of Second Corinthians on page 74.

Read 2 Corinthians 12:7-10. Read again 2 Corinthians 12:9.

The classical definition of humility

offered by Teresa of Ávila is to walk in the truth of who we are. This means accepting our weaknesses and our limitations as gifts of God as well as our strengths and talents.

ENTRY POINT:

Walking in the Truth

Given that definition, what does walking in the truth mean for you? How can you regard yourself as God regards you? How can you become more grateful for the way God has created you—in light of both your strengths and weaknesses? Meditate on these words and let them give you the courage to fulfill your calling as a minister of the new covenant. "My grace is sufficient for you, for my power is made perfect in weakness."

2 Corinthians 12:9

He said to me, "My grace is sufficient for you, for power is made perfect in weakness." So, I will boast all the more gladly of my weaknesses, so that the power of Christ may dwell in me.

Unity in

Christ

Read the introduction to the book of Galatians on page 75.

Read Galatians 2:20. Read again Galatians 2:20.

Imagine that someone has asked you to create a film of your life using this verse as the theme.

What scenes would you include to represent your life before

[
ENTRY POINT:

New Life at the Center
]

Jesus Christ came to live in you? After? What is different? Why? Whom would you cast for the major parts? What message do you hope your viewers will receive by watching your life? Pay attention to the details. Be open to ways in which you can thank God for the whole picture, even if some parts are painful to watch.

Galatians 2:20

it is no longer I who live, but it is Christ who lives in me. And the life I now live in the flesh I live by faith in the Son of God, who loved me and gave himself for me.

Read the introduction to the book of Ephesians on page 76.

Read Ephesians 4:14-16. Read again Ephesians 4:15-16.

Love is never lived out in isolation; rather it is integrated into every relationship. As we become rooted in the love of Jesus, we grow in integrity and truth.

[ENTRY POINT:

The Language of Love]

Lying denies God's love (see v. 25), while honesty inspires maturity and unity in any group of which we are members.

Prayerfully reflect on this scripture, inviting Jesus to guide you as you review the ways in which you speak with others. How do you speak to God, to those closest to you, and to others you meet throughout the day? How do you deal with difficult people? Try monitoring your speech for a few days, listening to how frequently you speak the language of love.

Ephesians 4:15-16

But speaking the truth in love, we must grow up in every way into him who is the head, into Christ, from whom the whole body, joined and knitted together by every ligament with which it is equipped, as each part is working properly, promotes the body's growth in building itself up in love.

Read the introduction to the book of Philippians on page 77.

Read Philippians 4:4-9. Read again Philippians 4:7.

What images and impressions does the word *peace* create for you?

The word *peace* has rich biblical connotations of reconciliation, wholeness, health, and

unity. The apostle Paul often greets fellow Christians with the words *grace* and *peace* (see Romans 1:7; 1 Corinthians 1:3; Galatians 1:3).

[**ENTRY POINT:** **Inventory of Peace**]

Read and ponder these words of scripture. Make two columns on a page of your journal. In one column list some of the things that rob you of peace. In the other column note some things that give you a sense of peace. Which column reflects the condition you find yourself in most often? How can this scripture passage guide you into greater peace?

Philippians 4:7

And the peace of God, which surpasses all understanding, will guard your hearts and your minds in Christ Jesus.

Day 4**

Read the introduction to the book of Colossians on page 78.

Read Colossians 1:15-20. Read again Colossians 1:15-20.

This beautiful hymn to Jesus Christ contains several wonderful images of his supremacy. List them using your own words. Then choose one of these images and meditate on it. Draw, paint, or fashion some sort of creative expression that reflects your experience of pondering this scripture. Keep it in your place of prayer to encourage you daily.

[
ENTRY POINT:

Motivated Living
]

Colossians 1:15-20

[Christ] is the image of the invisible God, the firstborn of all creation; for in him all things in heaven and on earth were created, things visible and invisible, whether thrones or dominions or rulers or powers—all things have been created through him and for him. He himself is before all things, and in him all things hold together. He is the head of the body, the church; he is the beginning, the firstborn from the dead, so that he might come to have first place in everything. For in him all the fullness of God was pleased to dwell, and through him God was pleased to reconcile to himself all things, whether on earth or in heaven, by making peace through the blood of his cross.

Read the introduction to the book of First Timothy on page 81.

Read 1 Timothy 6:3-16. Read again 1 Timothy 6:11.

Copy this verse on a piece of paper (or commit it to memory), then go outside and start walking. Pick a point on the horizon and as you walk

[
ENTRY POINT:

The Pursuit of Growth
]

toward it, prayerfully consider what activities mentioned throughout this letter will help you to "pursue" righteousness and godliness. Start running (or at least pick up the pace) for just a short while. What is the significance of the sense of urgency Paul conveys (see also 1 Corinthians 9:24-25)? Once you reach your destination, turn around and walk back, prayerfully considering Paul's words about growing in endurance. Are your legs tired? What makes you spiritually tired? How can you get in better shape spiritually?

1 Timothy 6:11

But as for you, man of God, shun all this; pursue righteousness, godliness, faith, love, endurance, gentleness.

Faith in

Community

Read the introduction to the book of Hebrews on page 85.

Read Hebrews 12:1-6. Read again Hebrews 12:1-2.

These verses are filled with action verbs.

Notice the verb phrases used to describe Jesus' actions on our behalf. Reflect on what Jesus has done for the sake of "the joy that was set before him":

> ENTRY POINT:
>
> # Therefore, Consider Jesus!

"endured the cross"
"disregarding its shame"
"has taken his seat."

Ponder the verb phrases that describe our response:

"lay aside"
"run with perseverance"
"looking to"
"consider him"
"not grow weary or lose heart."

How many of these action verbs capture the essence of your response to Jesus Christ? In what areas of your life would you like to deepen your faith? Spend some time in prayer with Jesus about that desire, repeating your need to him over the course of the next days and weeks.

Hebrews 12:1-2

Therefore, since we are surrounded by so great a cloud of witnesses, let us also lay aside every weight and the sin that clings so closely, and let us run with perseverance the race that is set before us, looking to Jesus the pioneer and perfecter of our faith, who for the sake of the joy that was set before him endured the cross, disregarding its shame, and has taken his seat at the right hand of the throne of God.

Read the introduction to the book of James on page 86.

Read James 5:13-20. Read again James 5:13-16.

Augustine once referred to the "walls of the church" as those braces and boundaries within which individuals who belong to the church are held. James

[
ENTRY POINT:
The Community of Care
]

closes his letter by describing those "walls" or means of grace—prayer, confession, healing, restoration— that benefit both the individual and the whole community. Recall an instance in which the church has provided for you in a time of specific need. Now think of less visible or dramatic ways in which your faith community has been a channel of God's grace in your life. In what ways can you become such a caring presence to a brother or sister, or to your congregation as a whole? Ask God to guide you in discerning and fulfilling that calling.

James 5:13-16

Are any among you suffering? They should pray. Are any cheerful? They should sing songs of praise. Are any among you sick? They should call for the elders of the church and have them pray over them, anointing them with oil in the name of the Lord. The prayer of faith will save the sick, and the Lord will raise them up; and anyone who has committed sins will be forgiven. Therefore confess your sins to one another, and pray for one another, so that you may be healed. The prayer of the righteous is powerful and effective.

Read the introduction to the book of First Peter on page 87.

Read 1 Peter 4:12-19. Read again 1 Peter 4:19.

Peter writes this letter to encourage his

readers to stand fast in the true grace of God. Pause and expectantly open your heart for a gift of true grace personally

[
ENTRY POINT:

True
Grace
]

underlined for you somewhere in this page of God's word. Now read slowly right through the passage, noting any special phrases, words, or verses that attract your attention.

Choose the one that draws you most strongly and return to it. Read that phrase or verse aloud, emphasizing different key words on each reading. Then quiet your spirit, and let the words nestle in a safe place within your heart. Let this gift of grace grow and bear fruit.

1 Peter 4:19

Therefore, let those suffering in accordance with God's will entrust themselves to a faithful Creator, while continuing to do good.

Day 4

Read the introduction to the book of Second Peter on page 88.

Read 2 Peter 2:17-20. Read again 2 Peter 2:19.

Peter does not mince words: "People are slaves to whatever masters them." Given all the examples he has just identified, we had better take his cautionary words seriously.

[
ENTRY POINT:

Slave or Free?
]

What controls you? What hinders your freedom and growth in Jesus Christ? Is it fear? the opinions of others? laziness? an addiction? an unforgiving spirit? greed? Or something else? Take time to let the Spirit reveal what enslaves you. Stand up and let your body feel as it would if bound with restricting ropes. Ask God to reveal the freedom Christ Jesus has won for you. As you see each rope being untied, move your body more and more freely and joyfully. End by assuming a posture that expresses your grateful commitment to true freedom.

2 Peter 2:19

They promise them freedom, but they themselves are slaves of corruption; for people are slaves to whatever masters them.

Read the introduction to the book of Revelation on page 93.

Read Revelation 21:1-7. Read again Revelation 21:3-5.

List the "old things" that hold you in bondage to your past—the hidden addiction that fills your heart with fear, the destructive habit that brings death to

[
ENTRY POINT:

All Things
New
]

your hopes and dreams, the unhealed memories that cause you sorrow, the damaged emotions that inflict pain on your spirit. Then, at each point, read and affirm Revelation 21:3. When you sense in your spirit the reality of God's loving presence with you, hear God say, "I am making all things new!" This exercise may be helpful to you as a daily discipline until the awareness of God's deliverance and healing permeates your heart and calms your spirit.

Revelation 21:3-5

And I heard a loud voice from the throne saying,
"See, the home of God is among mortals.
He will dwell with them;
they will be his peoples,
and God himself will be with them;
he will wipe every tear from their eyes.
Death will be no more;
mourning and crying and pain will be no more,
for the first things have passed away."
   And the one who was seated on the throne said, "See, I am making all things new." Also he said, "Write this, for these words are trustworthy and true."

Promises That Come True

Matthew writes this Gospel in the early church period when the church is predominantly Jewish. *Matthew frequently cites passages from the Old Testament that are fulfilled in the coming of Jesus the Messiah*, a watershed event in the long tradition of ancient Judaism. Matthew's intent is that those who read his Gospel, whether Jews or Gentiles, will see themselves as participants in the grand sweep of God's purposes in history. The coming of Jesus, says Matthew, is the culmination of all our waiting.

Matthew almost seems astonished *that God should become incarnate in Jesus Christ,* that people could see and hear and touch the Almighty God. As you read Matthew's Gospel, try to imagine yourself as a Jew in Gospel times. Your people have waited a thousand years for fulfillment. You have studied and remembered all the ancient prophecies and now, for the first time, they make sense. Suddenly, Almighty God is among your people. Emmanuel, *God is with us*, is present and active in the day-to-day life of the people—healing, feeding, teaching—bringing the word of God personally to the people of God.

As you read this Gospel, remember that *Jesus is still God with us*. He is God incarnate, with us in the Holy Spirit. What questions would you like to ask him? What would you like him to explain? What do you need him to do for you? What can you do for him? Make these questions the prayers of your heart.

Key Verse: "Do not think that I have come to abolish the law or the prophets; I have not come to abolish but to fulfill." —Matthew 5:17

What It Costs to Follow Jesus

What did it cost Jesus to do the work of his Father? ***What will it cost you to follow Jesus?*** You will find the answers to both questions in the Gospel of Mark. In this fast-paced narrative, the writer reveals what it cost Jesus to do this work: He was persecuted by the Pharisees (Mark 3:6); he had to address the bewilderment expressed by his family (3:21); he was rejected by his hometown crowd (6:3-4); he relinquished both his privacy (6:30-34) and material goods. When accused, he did not defend himself (14:61).

Mark also outlines the cost of following Jesus. As much as we prefer to identify ourselves with Jesus in his role of conquering king, ***we are also called to become like him as servants, reconciling those around us to God.*** Just as Jesus spoke the truth to the confused and the corrupt, so must we. Just as he addressed the physical needs of the crowds who followed him, so must we. Just as he sought to heal the broken places of people's hearts, so must we.

As you read this account, let the forward momentum of Mark's narrative instill within you a sense of urgency. ***The time to follow Jesus is now.*** As you read about Jesus' words and works, ask God what he is calling you to be and do. What do you need to know about the power of Jesus and the servant heart of Jesus in order to be conformed to his image for the sake of others?

Key Verse: "For the Son of Man came not to be served but to serve, and to give his life a ransom for many." —Mark 10:45

Life of Prayer, Life of Compassion

The Gospel of Luke *draws a portrait of Jesus the Savior, who brings the love of God to earth and draws the people of God to heaven.* Luke conveys a fascination with this Jesus, a man of both prayer and action, who could be continually mindful of God and yet be fully present with people as an attentive, empathetic healer. Jesus modeled perfect communication with his heavenly Father (the Lord's Prayer) and perfect compassion for those his culture considered outcasts (the parable of the good Samaritan).

Jesus' life and teachings reconcile some of the contrasts that exist within the spiritual life, blending spiritual with physical (6:24-27), feasting with fasting (5:33-35), compassion with confrontation (6:9), and solitude with community (6:12-16).

Jesus moved beyond the restrictions of Jewish society, welcoming anyone with a seeking heart and granting the forgiveness of God to those the "righteous" Jewish leaders had rejected (6:20-26; 21:1-4). He engaged women, as well as men, in ministry (8:1-3; 23:55–24:11). For the only Gentile Gospel writer, this was good news indeed, for Jesus brought reconciliation to the Gentile world.

Let the book of Luke help you *discover what it means to live an inward life of prayer and an outward life of compassion.* When you struggle to balance "doing" with "being," imitate Jesus Christ who practiced an ongoing rhythm of ministry and sabbath rest. How can you serve God in the same radical way? How can you maintain this rhythm in your personal life?

Key Verses: "Lord, teach us to pray." —Luke 11:1

"Which of these . . . was a neighbor? . . . Go and do likewise." —Luke 10:36-37

Living in the Light

The light is shining. It is a light that defies our ability to capture and define. *The light has a voice that speaks life to us.* The light has hands that hold and heal us. The light has a name—Jesus, the son of Mary, the Son of God.

The light became flesh. The light conquers darkness and turns death into life. Into situations as ordinary as a catering problem at a wedding or as deeply troubling as a death in the family, this light beams a transforming power. *When the light is present, everything is changed.* When the light is present in us, we are changed. We have eternal life. We are restored to the glory that our Creator God intended.

Many situations in the book of John may resemble your personal situations. As you read you might ask yourself, *"What is God doing here, and how can I be open to allow God to work within me?"* As you participate in a community of believers, you might ask, "What is God doing among us?"

The Gospel writer calls his community of Jews and non-Jews to follow the revolutionary—and sometimes unpopular—way of Jesus. *He shows that the way of Jesus is full of challenge and adventure*—full of the risk involved when we let go and trust. The way might be hard. But in Jesus we find grace and truth. In Jesus we will "have life, and have it abundantly!" (John 10:10). The writer urges us to dwell in the light of Jesus, so that *we might carry the death-defying love of God into the world.*

> *Key Verse:* The Word became flesh and lived among us, and we have seen his glory. . . . In him was life, and the life was the light of all people. —John 1:14, 4

The Good News Spreads under the Spirit's Guidance

This book might well be called "The Acts of the Holy Spirit." *From beginning to end the Spirit guides the spread of the gospel from Jerusalem to Rome itself.* Poured out on the day of Pentecost with "a sound like the rush of a violent wind" and "divided tongues, as of fire" (Acts 2:2-3), *the Spirit changes lives, alters plans, and transforms situations.* The Spirit empowers the early Christians to stand up to authorities, to face down mobs, to speak to hostile audiences, and to hold fast through suffering even to death—all for the sake of the good news of Jesus Christ. At the same time, the Spirit impels them far beyond their comfort zones into missions to the Samaritans and Gentiles and to people from all levels of society.

God's Spirit is active in our own lives—comforting, encouraging, strengthening, nudging. When have you felt led, like the early disciples, in a particular direction? When have you been the channel of God's love to someone else? When have you experienced a shower of grace when you needed it most? And when have you found resources of strength to do what seemed impossible? *You have experienced the work of the Spirit*, sent by Jesus Christ who "is exalted at the right hand of God, and [who has] received from the Father the promise of the Holy Spirit, . . . [and] has poured out this that you both see and hear" (2:33).

> **Key Verse:** "But you will receive power when the Holy Spirit has come upon you; and you will be my witnesses in Jerusalem, in all Judea and Samaria, and to the ends of the earth." —Acts 1:8

The Old Self and the New Self

Like a parent giving a gift to a child out of pure love, **God gives us the gift of salvation.** We do not have to do anything to deserve it, and we never could be good enough to earn it. In the book of Romans, the apostle Paul writes a treatise on the love of God. God's love is redeeming love, for every one of us is "under the power of sin" (3:9) and controlled by our human nature; we all "fall short of the glory of God" (3:23). **God initiates our redemption even before we are aware of our need of it.** In response to God's love, we are to turn our entire lives toward God so that, day by day, we are transformed—a process (5:1-4) that involves heart (2:29), mind (8:5-6), will (7:14-15), and actions (12:9-21)—as we become new persons who want what God wants (12:2).

Romans is a theological book, but it is also a realistic, practical discussion of how growing into fullness of life in Christ is a matter of mind, heart, and spirit. Throughout our inner struggles and our struggles with others, we are drawn by God's incredible love in Christ Jesus, which seeks us out and bears us along in the spiritual life. Nothing that we have done, or ever could do, can separate us from the love that God offers us in Christ Jesus our Lord.

Key Verse: But God proves his love for us in that while we still were sinners Christ died for us.
—Romans 5:8

First Corinthians

The Way of Love

In the apostle Paul's first letter to the Corinthians we encounter a missionary whose spirit is being transformed by the Holy Spirit. *Paul urges the people of the Corinthian church to be likewise transformed by the Spirit of God.* Paul admits that he is not a clever, eloquent orator but a childlike man who is "foolish" enough to preach the cross (1:17–2:16). *His servant posture cuts through the barriers of human factions to pull together a community of believers* who will proclaim in one voice that Jesus is Lord.

As you read Paul's letter and meditate on it, *imagine yourself in the presence of the apostle, a seasoned spiritual teacher who crowns his letter with the often-quoted essay on love.* Envision yourself telling Paul how hard it is for you to uphold this standard of love when you've had a spat with your spouse or felt misunderstood by your friend. Then turn your thoughts toward God in prayer. Ask God to help you cross the bridge between love in the abstract ("Of course I love people, but I can't stand my next-door neighbor!") and love in the concrete ("I know if I can learn to love my neighbor, then it won't be so hard to love other people"). *How might such prayerful interaction with what Paul writes help you to become more loving—and part of a more loving community in Jesus Christ?*

> **Key Verse:** Love is patient; love is kind; love is not envious or boastful or arrogant or rude. It does not insist on its own way; it is not irritable or resentful; it does not rejoice in wrongdoing, but rejoices in the truth. It bears all things, believes all things, hopes all things, endures all things.
> —1 Corinthians 13:4-7

Our Hope for New Life

One of the greatest obstacles facing us on the road to spiritual formation is our lack of appreciation for our infinite worth in the eyes of God. No matter what faults and failings may hamper us on our way home to our Father's house, God loves and forgives and welcomes us. *One of the gifts the apostle Paul gives his readers in this ardent and honest letter is a renewed sense of worthiness to minister in the name of Jesus Christ.* Paul applies correction but he also encourages his readers with an appraisal of their worth: They are "the aroma of Christ" (2:15); Christ's "ambassadors" (5:20); "the temple of the living God" (6:16). Paul's encouragement is not meant to produce pride in his readers but to remind them that "Jesus Christ is in [them]" (13:5). His spirit forms, reforms, and transforms us "into the same image from one degree of glory to another" (3:18).

The spirit of servanthood dies, as Paul sees it, when we try to become "super-apostles" (12:11), incapable of admitting that we are vulnerable, suffering, wounded creatures. *We can unlock the door to Christian service only with the key of our weaknesses.* Paul boasts of his "weaknesses, so that the power of Christ may dwell in [him]" (12:9).

As you read this letter, reflect on your ministry, whatever it may be. What do you think makes you competent to serve? *What are your strengths in Christ Jesus?* How are his strengths apparent through your weaknesses?

Key Verse: So if anyone is in Christ, there is a new creation: everything old has passed away; see, everything has become new! All this is from God, who reconciled us to himself through Christ, and has given us the ministry of reconciliation; that is, in Christ God was reconciling the world to himself, not counting their trespasses against them. —2 Corinthians 5:17-19

In Step with the Spirit

Parades are fun to watch, but it takes great concentration to march in one, especially if one is playing an instrument or carrying a flag. Bands designate a leader to set the proper cadence; the challenge for each band member is to stay in step—and not only when the band is in front of the viewing stand!

Paul's letter to the Galatians explores some of the difficulties that can cause Christians to get out of step as they follow Jesus Christ. Paul warns his readers against misunderstanding the role of the law, pursuing the dead end of human effort, and concentrating on external religious practice while neglecting their inner life.

Paul's letter is a refreshing message for the Galatians—and for us today: we don't have to struggle to be in control of our spiritual life. *God wants to guide us as we walk in step with the Holy Spirit so that we experience God's gracious freedom, guidance, and renewing joy.* As you read this letter, consider how your own lifestyle reflects the pace and power of the Holy Spirit. Be careful to notice those areas in which *God is calling you to get in step with the Spirit.*

Key Verse: If we live by the Spirit, let us also be guided by the Spirit. —Galatians 5:25

Rooted in Love

This letter to the Ephesians reminds us of the importance of roots. The health of a tree is dependent on the health of its root system. Roots reach deep into the soil to draw up the necessary nourishment to sustain the tree. Deep roots create stability and help the tree withstand the storms of life. Likewise, *when we are rooted in the powerful and boundless love of Jesus, we are prepared to face the challenges of living in a stormy world.*

This letter calls us to imitate God (5:1) as the means of developing healthy roots. That task is made possible by being in a community of love with other Christians (4:12-16). Furthermore, *our life is energized by the unconditional grace of Jesus rather than by our own human efforts (2:4-10).* Throughout this letter Paul (the attributed writer) offers prayers for his readers.

Pay attention to your own root system as you read and pray through Ephesians. *Pray that Jesus Christ will dwell within your heart more and more so that you are equipped to face the realities of life.* Consider the spiritual habits that have sustained you in the past. What new resources does this book offer to you? *How can you encourage others in the healthy planting of their roots deep into Jesus?*

Key Verse: I pray . . . that Christ may dwell in your hearts through faith, as you are being rooted and grounded in love. I pray that you may have the power to comprehend, with all the saints, what is the breadth and length and height and depth, and to know the love of Christ that surpasses knowledge. —Ephesians 3:16-19

Philippians

A Work in Progress

One of the characteristics of our contemporary culture is impatience. *Advances in technology encourage us to demand ever more in less time.* Unfortunately the continued pressure to rush everything has reduced our ability to wait for anything.

Some aspects of life, however, cannot be rushed. *Spiritual growth is no different than physical growth—both require time and great patience.* And when we experience growth, it is not always easy to detect. Progress sometimes seems meager. Perhaps that is why Christians have often been called a pilgrim people. *Our lives reflect the process of God's work more than any polished final product.*

In an age of instant gratification, the apostle *Paul proclaims a countercultural message.* He reminds us to be patient because God's work in us is not finished. Regardless of how long we have been concentrating on growing spiritually, *we are still beginners—and always will be*—until we reach heaven. Paul encourages us to press on and not give up. He emphasizes that *Christian maturity is a process of cooperating with God's presence and power in our lives.*

The message of Philippians is one of patience and hope. *Perhaps this book will renew your stagnant life or give you permission to seek excellence rather than perfection in all you do.* Regardless of where you find yourself, let these words inspire and invite you into deeper participation with the God who seeks to join you in spiritual partnership.

Key Verse: I am confident of this, that the one who began a good work among you will bring it to completion by the day of Jesus Christ. —Philippians 1:6

A Heart Set on God

Sometimes we fool ourselves, believing it is more difficult to live today than two thousand years ago. However the Christians of the first century faced equal or greater challenges to their faith. *The writer seeks to etch deeply into human hearts the truth that meaning and purpose do not come through any exclusive knowledge or superior spirituality.* Rather they are firmly established in the life of Jesus Christ, in whom God was pleased to dwell with all the divine fullness. Paul (the attributed writer) understands the serious crisis before his readers and seeks to weave these words into a fabric of practical guidance that clothes them with hearts that seek to focus on God. *In pondering these words of scripture, remember that the Bible uses the word* **heart** *to speak of mind, soul, and will.* How can the book of Colossians help you devote your life to God in all of these areas?

Key Verse: So if you have been raised with Christ, seek the things that are above, where Christ is, seated at the right hand of God. —Colossians 3:1

First Thessalonians

Waiting in Holiness

How often we wish for a friend who could give us spiritual help—not just casual advice but powerful counsel that would lead us to a closer relationship with God (2:12). The Christians of Thessalonica had such a friend in the apostle Paul. As he writes, *Paul is open about his affection for them, his longing to be their guide and religious instructor, and his pride in their success in living lives worthy of God's calling.* He is thrilled when Timothy reports that the faith and love Paul remembered as characteristic of them was still alive and flourishing among these faithful converts.

Paul's affection for the Thessalonians is so endearing that we might be reminded of a similar friend of our own. *Imagine returning home one day and finding a letter waiting in the mail from just such an old friend.* More than once you have wished you could sit and talk with this friend because he or she is a good listener and always knows just what to say to point you in the right direction.

Now imagine that this friend is someone like Paul, a person of considerable stature, who is keenly interested in the things you do, say, and think. In your last letter to this friend, what did you write about? What was weighing heavily on your heart? What joys did you share? Now how does this person's letter of response to you begin? *What concern seems most important?* What does your friend wish for you most of all? Read the book of First Thessalonians as if it were such a letter, written just for you and your faith community.

Key Verse: And may he so strengthen your hearts in holiness that you may be blameless before our God and Father at the coming of our Lord Jesus with all his saints. —1 Thessalonians 3:13

Second Thessalonians

A Life Worthy of God's Calling

The early church in Thessalonica is buzzing with predictions of Jesus' second coming. For some the fearful "end times" are troubling to contemplate. Others want only to wait passively for Jesus' return. The timing of this final event is uncertain, and many, in a state of paralysis, have given up their work and sit idly, awaiting the end of the world.

The author of this letter pointedly reminds his readers of who is in charge of all these things. The apostle Paul (the attributed writer) admonishes the Thessalonians not to be shaken but to have faith (2:2), remembering that God has chosen them.

Paul also confronts the destructiveness of fear and anxiety. They are to remain steadfast in their faith in the same way God is steadfast in God's love for them (2:15-16). Idleness only adds to the problem of worry, he says; and *he tells them to earn their own way (3:11-12) and live their lives as models of love and perseverance (3:5).*

Take time to reflect on your fears as you read Second Thessalonians. Which fears can you surrender to God? *How could a fuller measure of faith in God dispel your feelings of being overwhelmed and hopeless in your daily life?* What do you need to allow God to handle so that you can experience a turnabout in your ability to handle your fears? As you read this letter, *let yourself experience the presence of the One who can calm all your fears.*

Key Verse: To this end we always pray for you, asking that our God will make you worthy of his call and will fulfill by his power every good resolve and work of faith. —2 Thessalonians 1:11

Guidelines for Godliness

As the young pastor Timothy's mentor and friend, the apostle Paul (the attributed writer) writes to his "loyal child in the faith" with words of instruction and encouragement. *Timothy is pastoring a church that faces all the problems of a growing institution, not the least of which is keeping the church's love for Jesus Christ fresh and fervent (see Revelation 2:4).* Timothy has to manage the church's internal affairs such as personnel, structure, worship, and doctrinal struggles as well as to combat the continuing persecution and false teachings coming from outside and inside the church.

The book of First Timothy is primarily a call to godliness in the broadest sense. *Paul summons the congregation to godliness characterized by right doctrine, orderly worship, and holy relationships.* He addresses the mission of the church, the qualifications of leaders, and social concerns such as the care of widows.

To be godly is to imitate God in holiness; such a calling affects every part of our being, from our beliefs to our behavior, from our attitudes to our actions, and from our relationships to our worship. There isn't an element of human existence that isn't radically and profoundly altered by this call to Christian living that Paul refers to as godliness. Consider studying this book with a sheet of paper with the word *godliness* written at the top. Ask God to broaden your view of godliness and to remove the limits of your previous definition of the word. *Ask God to show you areas of your life that need to be anointed with new holiness.*

Key Verse: Pay close attention to yourself and to your teaching; continue in these things, for in doing this you will save both yourself and your hearers. —1 Timothy 4:16

Faithfulness under Pressure

Do you ever live through seasons in which the entire world seems bent on distracting you from God's calling? *As you seek to serve God, are you hampered by pressures and opposition?* If so, this letter will offer you profound encouragement. Whether your frustrations stem from the pressure of meeting many obligations, a feeling of weariness, or the experience of open opposition or ridicule, you will find empathy in Paul's and Timothy's experiences. Even as they face many of these same pressures, *Paul (the attributed writer) urges Timothy to persevere and remain faithful in his ministry.*

While most of the New Testament books are written to churches, this one is written to an individual. The situation in which Paul and Timothy find themselves is a veritable pressure cooker. Paul is in prison; the church is being persecuted; opposition is hot and fierce— even from those who call themselves Christians, and *Timothy is trying to stay true to his work in the midst of doctrinal confusion and hardship. Paul's letter is a stirring call to Timothy to remain faithful under pressure*, and its relevance has been proven in every generation.

Before you reflect on the specific teachings of this book, take a personal inventory of the challenges you have faced in serving God. *What has made it most difficult for you to fulfill a calling that you believe God has given you?* What is the biggest obstacle you currently face? Even as you confront your own struggles, prepare to be challenged and encouraged by Paul's words to his friend Timothy. Within these chapters you may find the keys to remaining faithful under pressure in your own life.

Key Verse: As for you, always be sober, endure suffering, do the work of an evangelist, carry out your ministry fully. —2 Timothy 4:5

Keeping Your Focus

Have you ever heard of the phrase "medical triage"? It refers to the practice of responding to natural or human disasters. *When the injured are so many and the physicians are so few, doctors and nurses must set priorities and work systematically*; otherwise they'd be overwhelmed and the situation would take much longer to bring under control.

On a spiritual level, this was the challenge Titus faced. He is left on the Mediterranean island of Crete to supervise a church planted among a particularly unruly people. The people of Crete were renowned for their malicious savagery and unrestrained passions. The idiom "to play the Cretan" meant to be a liar. Even Epimenides, one of Crete's own philosophers, chastised his homeland's moral character. These are the issues the writer takes up with Titus. By giving concrete advice in a clear framework, he seems to be saying, *"Don't be overwhelmed; stay focused; appoint qualified elders; challenge false teaching; pass on pure doctrine; and don't forget the importance of good deeds."*

This letter encapsulates the heart of true Christianity. Titus is overwhelmed, so the writer focuses only on what was most important. The challenge Titus faced long ago can result in something good for us today, for in this letter we are presented with the bedrock essence of our faith. *If you were left alone on an island to nurture a Christian church that had been planted in this culture, what would you emphasize?* How would you bring order? What would be your primary message?

Key Verse: I left you behind in Crete for this reason, so that you should put in order what remained to be done, and should appoint elders in every town, as I directed you. —Titus 1:5

A Plea for Reconciliation

This brief letter leads us into the middle of a difficult situation in the early church, one with parallels to our time. *Philemon was a first-century Christian living in Asia Minor.* His slave Onesimus escaped and met the imprisoned apostle Paul, who shared the gospel with him. Then Paul wrote this gracious and respectful letter encouraging Philemon to take back Onesimus—"no longer as a slave but . . . [as] a beloved brother" (v. 16).

Consider Philemon's options. *Should he free Onesimus and risk total chaos among the other slaves, who might fake conversions to win their freedom?* Should he punish Onesimus for running away? Should he return Onesimus to Paul? Or should he do what Paul suggests—welcome him home as a brother in Christ Jesus?

Welcoming people into our church communities after they have a change of heart can be a problem for us. If they have hurt us in the past, we may want to offer only the cold heart and closed fist of judgment. We may feel little eagerness to remove the stigma associated with their former reputations. After all, what will everyone else think if it looks like we are too easy on them?

But Paul takes a different approach by regarding other Christians as family members. Philemon is twice addressed as "brother." Apphia is a "sister." Because Onesimus is now a Christian, he too must be called "brother." *The apostle Paul encourages Philemon to do the hard thing— the right thing.* His letter asks us to do the same in the difficult relationships we may face in our own churches.

Key Verse: So if you consider me your partner, welcome him as you would welcome me.
—Philemon 17

A New and Better Way

Some people think that, in religious matters, tradition is all-important. Some, on the other hand, will have nothing to do with tradition; they forever want to be on the "cutting edge." Ideally, though, *the best of the new is that which grows from and builds on the depth and wisdom of the older traditions.*

For the writer of Hebrews, *the new covenant of Jesus Christ represented the fullness and completion of the revelation of God's love for humanity— the revelation God began with the old covenant.* In fact the Old Testament itself pointed to the unfolding of the new covenant of love in Jesus Christ—a new and superior way that would supersede the old.

As you read and meditate on these pages of scripture, notice how often they refer to Jesus' ministry as "superior to" or "better" than the ministry of the old covenant. *This book is about faith—God's faithfulness to us in giving us his Son, "the reflection of God's glory and the exact imprint of God's very being" (1:3),* and our faithful response to "looking to Jesus" (12:2). Open up any areas in your life in which you need to renew your trust and dependence on the promises of God and the provisions of Jesus Christ through the Holy Spirit.

> **Key Verse:** For this reason he is the mediator of a new covenant, so that those who are called may receive the promised eternal inheritance, because a death has occurred that redeems them from the transgressions under the first covenant. —Hebrews 9:15

Faith at Work

James could be said to have one objective in writing this letter: *to assist the churches to whom he writes to live well, that is, to work out their faith in good deeds and holy habits.* The straightforward, commonsense approach of this letter is refreshing, although *it might challenge and confront those who are comfortable in certain patterns of neglect or indifference toward others.* "Be doers of the word, and not merely hearers who deceive themselves" (1:22). "Understand this" (1:19). "You do well if you really fulfill the royal law" (2:8). These are the directives of a writer who is intent on reiterating or fleshing out the ancient words of the prophet Micah: "He has told you, O mortal, what is good; and what does the LORD require of you but to do justice, and to love kindness, and to walk humbly with your God?" (6:8).

As you contemplate these chapters, *let them be like candles lighting your soul, life, and habits.* How do they describe you or your church? How do they challenge you toward greater faithfulness in loving others? In the down-to-brass-tacks spirit of this letter, consider this question throughout: *What are specific and concrete ways in which I can respond to what I am reading?* Ask God to lead you into authentic behaviors and attitudes that—in challenging ways and ways that may stretch you perhaps—will put your faith to work.

Key Verse: But be doers of the word, and not merely hearers who deceive themselves.
—James 1:22

First Peter

Christians under Construction

Standing fast in the true grace of God transforms all of life. How simple it sounds. How seldom it is achieved! Peter (the attributed writer) knows this from personal experience. He knows how easy it is to wobble and fall. With a pastor's heart of compassion, he writes to Christians scattered in many places and facing a variety of tests and trials. *His warm, encouraging letter reminds them first of the blessings and hope they already have in Jesus Christ.* With that confident assurance they have every reason to be diligent in putting aside anything that could hold them back from full enjoyment of salvation.

The Christian life is no glowing dream world though. Peter is realistic. *Believers are to hold on in the midst of political challenges, slavery, abuse, questions from unbelievers, and suffering and pain.* Standing fast in these situations requires a clear sense of God's gracious presence. It also demands a disciplined commitment to living daily according to Jesus' example. Peter gives down-to-earth, specific guidance. *This is Christianity in everyday clothes.*

Even outright persecution is not to shake Jesus' followers from standing fast. As painful and puzzling as it is to suffer because of their faith, Peter's readers can be encouraged because of his gentle reminder that they share in Christ's sufferings.

Peter shows the care of a wise shepherd in the way he writes to his readers. His letter encourages us to care for others in the same way. *Humbled, disciplined, and strengthened by the power of Jesus Christ, we can stand firm in the amazing, true grace of God.*

Key Verse: I have written this short letter to encourage you and to testify that this is the true grace of God. Stand fast in it. —1 Peter 5:12

Listening for Truth

Would you prefer a godly life or a wallow in the mud (2:22)? Given the choice, most Christians would choose a godly life! Peter (the attributed writer) dramatically contrasts those two choices. He asserts that *everything needed for living a godly life has already been given us in Christ Jesus; it is simply waiting to be appropriated.* If this is the case, who would ever be diverted? "Well," says Peter, "plenty of people!" He pulls no punches. The examples he uses do not make for pleasant reading. Yet, shock tactics have their place in demanding our attention.

These particular shock tactics provide the basis for Peter's heartfelt exhortation that his readers be on the lookout for similar issues that might undermine their faith. *God is patient and leaves time for each generation of believers to identify the options and choose salvation and life.* But one day time will run out. How much better to be actively involved in growing in grace than to be caught unprepared.

The message of this letter is quite contemporary. Nothing has changed—God provides everything we need for a life of godliness. *We face the same challenge the early Christians did—to grow in our knowledge and experience of holiness in Jesus Christ.* Nothing has changed, either, in the human capacity to distort, scoff at, or simply disbelieve the grace of God. We, like the recipients of Peter's letter, have been forewarned: stay away from the mud and discover the green pastures of godliness!

Key Verse: Grow in the grace and knowledge of our Lord and Savior Jesus Christ. —2 Peter 3:18

Living in Love

John's letter paints a panoramic portrait of love the way God sees it. As we read and pray through these brief but powerful pages, two facets of biblical love seem to stand out. First, *before we are able to practice or walk in love, we must have some awareness of its nature.* Love is grounded in God (4:8, 16) and is most clearly depicted in Jesus Christ, who sacrificially offered his life for us (3:16; 4:10). *John calls us to the same kind of sacrificial love in which our actions align with our words in truth (3:18).*

Second, the apostle John (the attributed writer) connects love with obedience. *Obedience is our joyful response to the love of Jesus Christ, which allows us to live in him and he in us* (2:3-5; 2 John 5-6). We are commanded to walk in love not only when it is convenient for us but each day because we are children of God (5:2).

As you reflect on these words, *review your experience of God's incredible love for you.* Think about how you express that love to others. And as you ponder this message, prayerfully *ask God to help you to see God more clearly, love God more dearly, and follow God more nearly* as you mirror divine love day by day.

Key Verse: God is love, and those who abide in love abide in God, and God abides in them.
—1 John 4:16

Walking in Love

Biblical love is contagious! *Love is a dynamic, blazing flame that awakens us by its power, passion, and reality.* However, our life experiences remind us that not everyone is inspired by the integrity of love. As strange as it may seem, some are equally motivated by error. This brief letter summarizes the battle being waged within the believer between walking in love and walking in error. *True love—expressed in obedience—produces the richness of delight in God (v. 6).* But walking in error and heresy yields the emptiness of deception and danger (vv. 7-11). John (the attributed writer) alerts us to the same potential pitfalls today. As you read this short book, don't underestimate the importance of its message. *Whom or what do you welcome into your life?* Do those people, activities, and experiences encourage you to walk in love or in error?

Key Verse: This is the commandment just as you have heard it from the beginning—you must walk in it. —2 John 6

Walking in Truth

What a startling comparison John (the attributed writer) paints on the canvas of this book of holy scripture. ***Two specific individuals are mentioned by name to illustrate the importance of personal character.*** Diotrephes, who is characterized by self-love, exhibits an inhospitable attitude that ravages the Christian community (vv. 9-10). In stark contrast is Demetrius, whose reputation for truthful living is affirmed by everyone (v. 12). His life is marked by integrity, and John holds him up as a fitting model for his readers. It is evident from John's words that ***walking in truth is more than speaking the correct words. It requires the formation of character that is honest and is worthy of God.*** Indeed John's third letter could serve as a New Testament counterpoint to Micah's great ethical summary of the law: "He has told you, O mortal, what is good; and what does the LORD require of you but to do justice, and to love kindness, and to walk humbly with your God?" (6:8).

Key Verse: I have no greater joy than this, to hear that my children are walking in the truth.
—3 John 4

Standing Firm

This little book is short, sharp, and salutary. *Jude sets out to write an enthusiastic letter about the wonders of salvation but finds himself writing strong, stern words instead.* He is motivated by love of God and love for his readers.

Jude (the attributed writer, who is said by tradition to be the brother of Jesus as well as his servant) burns with passion for the purity of the faith; he can't bear to see it undermined. But that is exactly what is happening, and a warning must be issued. With anguish and energy Jude startles his readers into taking notice. At the beginning and end of the letter, Jude speaks of the mercy, peace, love, power, and security that are available in Jesus Christ. In the middle of the letter, Jude gives graphic examples of the awful possibility of perverting what Jesus offers. Though the examples Jude gives certainly would have evoked powerful memories for his original readers, some of them may seem irrelevant to us in our culture and our time. We can't escape the significance of this letter however. God's Spirit, who inspired Jude's letter, asks us to consider what might pervert God's grace in our day. *What behavior, lifestyle, attitudes, or destructive talk do we need to address?* Do we need to wake up? After all, we are nearer to the "last time" than Jude's readers were! May his passionate words kindle the fire of love in our hearts. Be warned. Take action. *Keep yourself in the love of God.*

Key Verse: Keep yourselves in the love of God; look forward to the mercy of our Lord Jesus Christ that leads to eternal life. —Jude 21

Revelation

A Kingdom of Priests

The book of Revelation paints sweeping landscapes of two worlds: the sinful world that will pass away ("'Fallen, fallen is Babylon the great!'" [18:2]) and, in contrast, a new world established in Jesus Christ that is the true home of all believers ("I saw the holy city, the new Jerusalem, coming down out of heaven from God" [21:2]).

There are many interpretations of this apocalyptic book. Some interpret it as exclusively futuristic and place the events of the book in the end times. This view, however, avoids the call to radical discipleship at the heart of John's vision. *Revelation can be seen as a map of the Christian's spiritual journey from citizenship in Babylon to citizenship in the new Jerusalem.* Babylon represents all the destructive, self-centered, dehumanizing effects of sin in this world, while Jerusalem represents the healing and liberation of new life in Christ. Redeemed in the blood of the Lamb of God, *believers find a new identity in Jesus Christ and become "priests" of God* who represent the presence of God in the fallen world.

As you meditate on John's vision, try to put aside all your preconceptions about Revelation and listen to the voice of the Spirit speaking to your heart about your true life as a "priest" in God's kingdom. *Listen for God's call for you to become what you were created to be—a beloved child created in the image of God, a member of God's kingdom.* Let the love of God become evident in you as you live in profound integrity and wholeness.

Key Verse: To him who loves us and freed us from our sins by his blood, and made us to be a kingdom, priests serving his God and Father, to him be glory and dominion forever and ever. Amen.
—Revelation 1:5-6
